JAMAICAN CAKES

MiQuel Marvin Samuels

Copyright © 2015 MiQuel Marvin Samuels

All rights reserved.

ISBN-13: 978-9769581012 (Liberate PEOPLE)
ISBN-10: 9769581011

INTRODUCTION

Buy these cookbooks: JAMAICAN DINNERS, JAMAICAN BREAKFASTS, and JAMAICAN SOUPS. Now here is bake-book, JAMAICAN CAKES. This book will give you Caribbean and Jamaica's perspective on cakes, buns, breads, and puddings.

In this cookbook, I will give you pictures and recipes with instructions of the most popular Jamaican cakes people are eating today. Few of the recipes will be authentic, others traditional Jamaican. By using coconut milk and healthier oil, in small ways, I am advocating new healthy alternative baking Jamaican cakes.

Nothing is best, than guide, and formula for baking great cakes. Instructions in this bake-book are clear and precise. You will have no trouble to understand the recipes. To be sure, the information is easy to grasp, I provided a website with video tutorials. Visit jamaicandinners.com if you are unsure.

Enjoy, baking Jamaica's cakes in your own oven. Surprise your friends from Jamaica. Surprise your spouse from Jamaica. Buy this book now. Start practicing my methods. They will love you. Take a big slice of Jamaica for yourself. Here is Jamaica's baking recipes, and my secrets.

CONTENTS

	Acknowledgments	I
1	Angel Cake	Pg 1
2	Banana Bread | Coconut Milk verse Cows' Milk	Pg 3
3	Birthday Cake	Pg 9
4	Black Forest Layered Cake	Pg 12
5	Caribbean Pineapple Cream Cheese	Pg 16
6	Caribbean Plain Cake	Pg 19
7	Caribbean Pound Cake	Pg 21
8	Carrot Cake Peanut Frosting	Pg 23
9	Cassava Pudding	Pg 26
10	Cheesecake	Pg 29
11	Chocolate Layered Cake	Pg 31
12	Chocolate Raspberry Marble Cake	Pg 34
13	Christmas Cake (Fruit Cake)	Pg 37
14	Coconut Peanut Cake	Pg 40
15	Coconut Pudding	Pg 43
16	Coffee Cake (Caribbean method)	Pg 46
17	Coffee Chocolate Cheesecake	Pg 48
18	Cornbread (Caribbean method)	Pg 51

	Acknowledgments	vi
19	Cornmeal Pudding	Pg 53
20	Easter Bun with Stout (method#1 of 3)	Pg 56
21	Easter Bun non-alcoholic (method#2 of 3)	Pg 59
22	Jamaican Hardough Bread	Pg 62
23	MiQuels' Ginger Cake	Pg 64
24	Old Fashion Easter Bun (method#3 of 3)	Pg 66
25	Pineapple Upside Down Apple Shortcake	Pg 69
26	Rum and Raisins Cake	Pg 72
27	Spice Bun	Pg 74
28	Sponge Cake	Pg 77
29	Sweet Potato Pudding	Pg 80
30	Toto Cake	Pg 83
31	Tutti-Fruitti Cake	Pg 85
32	Types of Butters, Oils and Shortening	Pg 87
33	Measurements Equivalents	Pg 90
34	Conclusion | Oven Conversion Chart	Pg 91

ACKNOWLEDGMENTS

My mother Beverly Lyseight and her twin sister Norma Lyseight-Doswell exposed me to the knowledge of baking, from a child.

Innovation made this bake-book possible. I admit using digital camera, computer, photo-shop, Microsoft, and grammar editing software to complete this book.

I retained from the internet nutriments and benefits on cow's milk, coconut, butter, and oils. They are correct, but please research on your own for assurance. I am not a scientist nor am I doctor.

Although Jamaica's grammar language is United Kingdom's English, my writing style is American grammar.

Thank God, for grace, encouragement, endurance, and strength. It took divine intervention and people like you to make Jamaican Cakes bake-book possible.

I did the cookbooks graphics, designing, recipes, and photographs, MiQuel Marvin Samuels baked and wrote all recipes. He edited, published this bake book.

It is my divine responsibility that I must complete series of cookbooks, to have precise recipes and clear instructions of the most popular Jamaican foods; people are eating each day. Jamaican cakes bake-book has healthy alternative recipes to prepare and bake Jamaica's cakes.

1

ANGEL CAKE

I used a plastic tube container when I baked this angel cake, not a good experienced. Use a two-pieces metal tube baking-pan for best results.

Angel cake is delicious accompaniment with cheese. My Grandmother loved eating a sliced in the morning with her mint tea. My Grandfather loved eating a sliced of angel cake with bush tea. I remembered my families baking.

ANGEL CAKE

Ingredients:

- 1 ½ cups of sugar (granulated white)
- 12 large eggs' white (room temperature)
- 1 ¼ cups of flour (all purpose, sifted first, or use cake flour)
- 1 tablespoon lime juice
- 1 teaspoon nutmeg extract
- 2 tablespoons vanilla extract
- 1 tablespoon almond flavoring
- ½ teaspoon of sea salt (any)
- ½ teaspoon cream of tartar

Instructions:

1. You need 10 inches two pieces angel cake tube pan. Sift flour and half the sugar together; put aside for later, and then separate eggs' yolk from white.
2. Put egg whites in bowl, and beat on medium low speed until foams.
3. Add salt, almond flavoring, nutmeg, vanilla extract, limejuice, and the cream of tartar. Use salt if you do not have "cream of tartar."
4. While it beats, add the other half sugar gradually, sure it is dissolves into egg whites. Do not allow over beat.
5. Beat on medium low speed until stiff, glossy with a peak form.
6. It takes a while to peak, put a little between your fingers; you must not feel any sugar grain.
7. The best time to preheat oven at 180°C or 350°F is now, 10 minutes before baking.
8. After that, use a rubber spatula or big balloon whisk.
9. Sift the flour in three parts over the beaten egg whites.
10. Add the flour gradually by folding; (you do not want batter to deflate.) Do not over fold.
11. Now, Use the rubber spatula to add the batter to the two-pieces angel cake baking pan. (Remember do not grease it.)
12. Bake for 45 minutes. Keep oven closed within set time for all recipes.
13. To avoid the cake from deflating turned two empty loaf-baking pans upside down on a surface. Then flip cake and lay in middle between the loaf pans.
14. After cools, removed cake by using small metal spatula or a knife score around sides loosens cake. Flip and removed cake. Slice for 24 people! Keep in refrigerator for 5 days freshness.

2

BANANA BREAD

Many countries in our world love the delicious taste of banana bread. The name is lovely; Say it, BANANA BREAD!

The first time I tasted banana bread, is when my mother baked it. The banana bread looked like that picture. I wanted the whole loaf. Nevertheless, banana bread and rock cakes, sold out fast at our home bakery.

BANANA BREAD

Ingredients:

- 4 cups flour (all-purpose)
- 1 teaspoon baking soda
- 1 teaspoon baking powder
- ½ teaspoon sea salt
- 1 cup butter (real flavored butter makes delicious cake)
- 1 ¼ cups brown sugar
- 4 eggs, beaten
- 4 ½ cups mashed over ripening bananas (equals 10 large bananas)
- 1 teaspoon cinnamon powder
- 1 teaspoon of nutmeg (grated)
- 2 tablespoons white rum (optional)

Instructions:
1. Preheat oven to 350 degrees F. (175 degrees C).
2. Lightly grease two 9 x 5 inches loaf-pan. Alternatively, 13 x 5.5 inches with smaller baking pan. Peel mashed over ripening bananas smooth.
3. In a large bowl, combine flour, baking powder, soda, grated nutmeg and salt. In a separate bowl, cream together butter and brown sugar.
4. Stir in eggs and mashed bananas until blends properly. Beat eggs first!
5. Stir banana mixture into flour mixture; stir dissolving. Pour batter into prepared loaf pan. Lifted dropped, few times releases bubbles.
6. Bake in preheated oven for 60 to 65 minutes, until a toothpick inserted into center of the loaf comes out cleaned. Allow cooling!
7. After that, removed cake by using small metal spatula or a knife; score around sides loosens cake. Flipped and placed on a plate, then slice for 24 people. Keep sealed in refrigerator for 5 days freshness.

COCONUT MILK BENEFITS, TRUTH ABOUT COW'S MILK

Coconut is a super-food. It combines fatty acids have profound positive effects on health, which includes fat loss, better brain function and various other amazing benefits. The health benefits of coconut oil confirmed in human studies experimentally.

Coconut Oil Contain unique Combination of Fatty Acids with powerful medicinal properties, Coconut oil is not use much now, so it was in the past, because it contains, "saturated fat." True, coconut oil is one of the richest sources of, "saturated fat" known to man. It is almost 90% of, "fatty acids" in it - saturated.

This important information, data shows saturated fats are harmless. Many massive studies that include hundreds of thousands of people proving "artery-clogging" were a myth. Additionally, coconut oil does not contain your saturated fats, such as products you would find in processed food, cheese, and other foods. There is no so-called Medium Chain Triglycerides (MCTs) – which are fatty acids of a medium length. Most of the fatty acids in the diet products are long-chain fatty acids, the medium-chain fatty acids in coconut oil metabolized differently.

Going straight to liver from digestive tract or turned into ketone bodies, giving quick energy. Having therapeutic effects on brain, disorders like epilepsy, and Alzheimer's disease. Coconut oil contains, medium chain triglycerides, which metabolized differently and can have therapeutic effects on several brain disorders.

People on that eat plenty coconut is the healthiest on earth. Coconut is exotic food in the Western world place and Caribbean Islands like Jamaica. Primarily health conscious people, such as Rastafarians and me, consume coconut. These people are in excellent health, with no evidence of heart disease.

Coconut oil increases energy and it expenditure. It will help you burn body fat. Some people think obesity is matters of calories. Yes! However, where the calories came from obesity persons are eating.

Below in oil chapter you will read and learn what is trans-fat. The medium-chain triglycerides (MCTs) in coconut oil increases energy, comparing calories from longer chain fats. One study found that 15-30 grams of MCTs per day increased 24 hours energy expenditure by 5%, totaling about 120 calories per day. Medium chain triglycerides in coconut oil increase

24 hours of energy by 5%; potentially leading to significant weight loss over long term.

The Lauric acid in coconut oil kills bacteria, viruses and fungi, helping to stave off infections running away from pathogens. Almost 50% of the fatty acids in coconut oil are the 12-carbon Lauric Acid. When coconut oil enzymatic-ally digested, it forms a monoglyceride called monolaurin. Lauric acid and monolaurin both kills harmful pathogens like bacteria, viruses and fungi. For example, these substances show to kill the bacteria Staphylococcus Aureus (a very dangerous pathogen). In addition, the yeast Candida Albicans, a common source of yeast infections in humans. The fatty acids and breakdown products in coconut oil can kill harmful pathogens, potentially helping to prevent infections.

Coconut oil satisfies hunger, making you eat less bad foods. The fatty acids metabolized, the ketone bodies have an appetite reducing effect. Studies showed varying amounts of medium and long chain triglycerides fed to six healthy men. The men eating the most MCTs ate 256 fewer calories per day, on average.

Another study in 14 healthy men discovered that those who ate the most MCTs at breakfast ate significantly fewer calories at lunch. If this effect were to persist over the long term, it could have a dramatic influence on body weight over a period of several years. The fatty acids in coconut oil can significantly reduce appetite, which may positively affect body weight over the long term.

The fatty acids in coconut oil turn into ketones, which reduce seizures. Coconut has ketogenic, a very low carbohydrate, very high fat. Now they are studying to treat various disorders. It might be the best therapeutic application treating drug-resistant epilepsy in children.

This diet involves eating very little carbohydrates and large amounts of fat, leading to greatly increased concentrations of ketone bodies in the blood. For some reason, this diet can dramatically reduce the rate of seizures in epileptic children, even those who have not had success with multiple different types of drugs. See, why I love the coconut, sometime I eat it raw. The MCTs in coconut oil goes to the liver and turned into ketone bodies; used in epileptic patients to induce ketosis while allowing for a bit more carbohydrates in the diet. The MCTs in coconut oil increase blood concentration of ketone bodies, which reduce seizures in epileptic children.

Coconut oil improves blood cholesterol levels and lower risk for heart disease. Coconut oil is loaded with saturated fats, which actually do not harm the blood lipid profile like previously thought. Saturated fats raise HDL (the good) cholesterol and change the LDL cholesterol to a benign subtype.

Studies with few women, shows coconut oil reduced total and LDL cholesterol while increasing HDL compared to soybean oil. Rat studies states coconut oil reduces triglycerides, total and LDL cholesterol; increases HDL and improves blood coagulation factors and antioxidant status. This improvement in cardiovascular risk factors should theoretically lead to a reduced risk of heart disease over the long term. Therefore women eat plenty coconut. Buy coconut break and eat it raw three per a day. Studies in both humans and rats show that coconut oil improves important risk factors like Total, LDL and HDL cholesterol, which may translate to a reduced risk of heart disease.

Coconut oil protects hair from damage, moisturize skin and function as sunscreen. I use nothing but raw coconut oil on my skin. Using it improve health and appearance of their skin and hair. Studies on individuals with dry skin show that coconut oil can improve the moisture and lipid content of the skin. Coconut oil protective against hair damage and one study shows effectiveness as sunscreen, blocking about 20% of the sun's ultraviolet rays.

Coconut oil can be used has mouthwash in process called oil pulling, which can kill some of the harmful bacteria in the mouth, improve dental health and reduce bad breath, research stated. Coconut oil is effective skin moisturizer and protects against hair damage as well. It a mild form of sunscreen and can be use as mouthwash.

Fatty acids in coconut oil boost brain function in Alzheimer's patients. Alzheimer's disease is the most common cause of dementia worldwide and occurs primarily in elderly individuals. Alzheimer's patients appear reduce abilities to use glucose for energy in certain parts of the brain. Ketone bodies can supply energy for the brain and researchers have speculated that ketones provides an alternative energy source for these malfunctioning cells and reduce symptoms of Alzheimer's. That is good news.

A 2006 study concludes consumption of medium chain triglycerides led to immediate improvement in brain function in patients, with milder forms of Alzheimer's. These important findings shows, medium chain triglycerides, are potential therapeutic agents in Alzheimer's disease. The fatty acids in coconut oil can increase blood levels of ketone bodies, supplying energy for the brain cells of Alzheimer's patients and relieving symptoms.

Coconut oil helps eliminate dangerous fat in your abdominal cavity for a man who needs to lose weight. Coconut oil reduces appetite and increase fat burning. Coconut oil effectively reduces abdominal fat lodges in the abdominal cavity and around organs. It is where the most dangerous fat that highly associated with many diseases.

Waist circumference is easily measured and is a marker for fat in the abdominal cavity. A studies on women abdominal obesity, was given supplements with coconut oil 30 ml (1 ounce), per day lead to a significant reduction in both BMI and waist circumference in a period of 12 weeks.

Twenty obese males reduced waist circumference of 2.86 cm (1.1 inches) after 4 weeks of 30 ml (1 ounce) of coconut oil per day. They lost abdominal fat simply by adding coconut oil to their diet. I use coconut milk and oil to do everything with my body, my best decision, many options, and your choice.

TRUTH ABOUT COW'S MILK

Cow's milk is a complete source of protein. It has eight grams of protein and 12 grams of carbohydrates per cup. Cow's milk on its own — without fortification — has 300 milligrams of calcium, one cup of milk has half of the recommended daily allowance of B12.

Cow's milk has lactose, so causing gastrointestinal or digestive problems for people who have deficiency to lactase enzyme. There is no fiber in cow's milk, the fat variable, it include saturated fat. There is less fat in lower-fat versions milk, such as one percent, skim, or 2 percent milk. Cow's milk has about double the amount of protein as soymilk. Such as Potassium, phosphorous, added vitamin D and other nutrients, this is in other foods.

Cow's milk fortified with vitamin D, you need vitamin D to absorb calcium. Soy and cow's milk have different types of protein. The protein in cow's milk is casein. Our bodies processes and use the nutrients from animals' sources better than plant sources. Yes, you can be vegetarian, but if you know me, meat protein is best for the human brain. Soymilk is a bad option for vegetarian people. Soymilk is the best substitute out there when it comes to milk substitutes: Almond milk, rice milk, or hemp milk. However, they cannot replace cow's milk. They are very low in protein. I drink coconut milk for the essence of drinking cow's milk. You can eat nuts to add protein for your diet. The human's stomach is not design to digest cow's milk effectively.

3

BIRTHDAY CAKE

This is Jamaica's traditional birthday cake, same look, taste, and feel.

BIRTHDAY CAKE

Ingredients:

- 3 cups of flour (all purpose or cake flour)
- 2 tablespoons of baking powder
- 1 teaspoon of sea salt
- 1 cup of butter (real flavored butter makes delicious cake)
- 2 cups of sugar (brown or white)
- 4 eggs (lighter cake if beaten)
- 1 cup of coconut milk, or cow's milk
- ¼ teaspoon of white vinegar (use to distort spoilage with coconut milk only)
- 2 teaspoons of vanilla extract

ICING FOR FROSTING: (divide proportion, then add colors or flavor)

- 4 cups icing sugar (powdered sugar)
- 1 cup shortening (room temperature)
- 4 tablespoons of limes' juice (optional)
- 6 tablespoons of white rum (to preserve it; optional not for children)
- 6 tablespoons of water (use more or less to soften icing)
- 1 teaspoon of food coloring for each (of any color), or molasses, coffee, or chocolate powder

Instructions:

1. Cut two greased papers to size baking pan, mine is 8.5 to a 9 inches diameter baking-pan.
2. Greased the baking pan, and lay the papers. Put aside.
3. You can prepare this Jamaican birthday cake two ways.
4. a), after baking and cooled, lay icing all on one large cake, or cut half horizontally into two layers. This method baking time is 55 minutes.
5. b), or, bake two smaller cakes, lay icing in the middle and all over, making two layered cake. Use 7 inches baking pan, and then put half the dough in each pan. Bake for 30 to 35 minutes.
6. Sift the flour with the baking powder, and salt. Put aside.
7. Now, dice the room temperature butter, and add the sugar. Use a wooden spoon and cream together in bowl.
8. Next, beat the eggs with vanilla extract, and add coconut milk with a drop of white vinegar. (Using the white vinegar distorts spoilage).

9. Cream the egg mixture to the butter mixture.
10. Then, add the flour mixture to the creamed butter.
11. Use a mixer, or a wooden spoon, beat the dough properly.
12. After that, pour dough into baking pan.
13. Lift and dropped, two to six times releases the air bubbles.
14. Bake for 55 minutes in a preheated oven at 350 degrees F., using 8.5 to 9 inches baking pan, Do not over oven within set time.
15. If baking separate cakes use two 7-inches baking pans, and then divide dough equally. Bake for 35 minutes.
16. Insert toothpick if cleaned, finished; allow cooling before you remove cake from the pan.
17. Flip baking pan with cake over, use your palm to hold the surface of the cake, removed the greased papers, place a plate on the cakes' bottom, and then flipped upright. Slice serving 24 children. Keep sealed in refrigerator for 5 days freshness, but first add frost.

Icing or Frosting Birthday Cake:

1. Place cake on icing board or plate.
2. Sift icing sugar fine, and then add ingredients. Beat properly!
3. Divide icing mixture into certain amount; add different colors. Use for writing, lining borders, for making roses, etc.
4. Base cakes' surface; spread icing.
5. Next, use decorating icing tools to design edges and letters
6. Put icing in the middle for double-layered cakes. If need cut horizontally curving top off bottom layered cake.

Jamaican authentic birthday cake, it is traditional.

4

BLACK FOREST CAKE

The only reason black forest cake in this book is because we loved eating it. Many bakeries in Jamaica bake to sell their own black forest cake.

Although black forest layered cake is expensive, people buy still because it is delicious. My secret formula homemade recipe for heavy whipped cream is below.

BLACK FOREST CAKE

Ingredients:

- 1 cup butter (room temperature)
- 2 ¼ cups sugar (brown or granulated)
- 4 eggs
- 2 ½ cups all-purpose flour
- 1 cup cocoa powder (natural and unsweetened)
- ½ teaspoon baking powder
- 1 teaspoon baking soda
- 1 teaspoon of cinnamon powder
- ½ teaspoon of nutmeg (grated)
- 1 teaspoon vanilla extract
- 1 ½ cups coconut milk, or cow's milk

Ingredients for filling:

- 3 cups heavy whipping cream (chilled to room temperature)
- ½ cup icing sugar
- ½ cup (Kirsch), red wine, or cherry brandy (use to sprinkle between layers; optional)
- 2 cans cherry pie filling (use place on layers and top)
- Milk chocolate curls or shavings, for garnish. (I used regular chocolate bar with nuts and mashed it).
- Maraschino cherries or sweet cherries, for garnish; optional

TO MAKE HEAVY WHIPPED CREAM:

- 3 cups of heavy whipped cream
- ½ cup of icing sugar

(Advice to you about the filling: Heavy Whipping Cream is expensive, do the following below to make your own.)

- 3 cups of cow's milk, or coconut milk with,
- 1 to 2 tablespoons of food corn starch, and add
- ½ cup of icing sugar.

Beat with an electric mixer until foamed heavily.

Instructions:

1. Preheat oven to 350 degrees F or 180 degrees C, 10 minutes before baking.
2. Line 9 inches (23 cm) cake pan with greaseproof or two non-stick papers.
3. Use an electric mixer; beat the softened butter with sugar until white and smooth.
4. Add one egg at a time break in separate container first, mix properly between two eggs.
5. Sift add flour, cocoa powder, baking powder, grated nutmeg, and baking soda.
6. Next add, vanilla extract, and coconut milk, or cow's milk, or butter milk, and mix until the batter is smooth.
7. Pour dough into cake pan and bake at 350 degrees F. just until set in the middle, 60 minutes or 10 minutes more. Insert toothpick in center should come out cleaned and not wet. Although Jamaicans like your cake a bit dry. Do not over-bake!
8. After cake cools, use a long serrated knife to cut the cake horizontally into three equal layers. It is easier to cut if kept refrigerated for a few hours. Alternatively, be creative I used long sharp knife to cut layers.

Black forest cake filling and frosting:

1. Drain cherry pie filling in a colander to removed most of the thickened juices.
2. Beat the whipping cream with confectioners' sugar until it thickens.
3. Using a vegetable peeler, shave chocolate, refrigerate until the cake is ready for assembling.

Assembling:
1. Sprinkle each layer of the cake with Kirshwasser, or Cherry Brandy, or any cherry red wine.
2. Place one cake layer on a large plate, dish, or icing plate.
3. Spread about one fifth of the whipped cream on each layer, and sprinkle half of the diced cherries on top of the whipped cream mixture.
4. Add the second cake layer.
5. Spread one fifth of the whipped cream mixture, diced cherries on top the second layer.
6. Add the third cake layer.
7. Spread one fifth of the whipped cream mixture on top and one fifth on the sides.
8. Gently press; sprinkle chocolate curls on the sides and/or on top of the cake.

Variations:
1. You may substitute the cherry pie filling with cherry jam. In that case, first spread the jam on the cake layers, then whipped cream mixture on top.
2. You may bake three separate cakes instead of one. In that case, baking time is 25 to 35 minutes; slice serving 24 people.

Keep black forest cake sealed in refrigerator for two weeks freshness.

5

CARIBBEAN PINEAPPLE CREAM CHEESECAKE

You must know the ingredients for baking Caribbean pineapple cream cheesecake is expensive for the average person like me in Jamaica.

That is why I used substituted ingredients in this recipe. In addition, allowing me to find a taste for Jamaican cheesecake. The crust of my cheesecake tastes like sandwich biscuits. The cream crackers worked.

CARIBBEAN PINEAPPLE CREAM CHEESECAKE

Ingredients:

CRUST:

- 1 ½ cups of Jamaican cream crackers crumble, or Graham cracker
- 6 tablespoons of butter (melted)
- ¼ cup of sugar (granulated)
- ¼ teaspoon of nutmeg (grated)

TOPPING:

- ½ cup of sour cream
- 3 teaspoons of pineapple's juice (from canned pineapple)
- 1 tablespoon of sugar (granulated)

FILLING:

- 1 (20 ounces) canned crushed pineapple
- 1 teaspoon of vanilla extract
- 1 pound of cream cheese
- 2/3 cup of sugar (granulated)
- 4 eggs (large, and beaten slightly)

Instructions: **CRUST:**

1. First, greased an 8 inches spring-form pan.
2. Mix crumbled crackers with sugar and butter in a bowl large enough.
3. Next, pour the mixture into the greased spring-form pan.
4. Use your fingers to press bottom and sides shape crust.
5. Now, put the spring-form pan with the compressed crust in refrigerator for 5 to 8 minutes. (That will get the crust firm)

Caribbean pineapple cream cheesecake
FILLING:

1. Now, add eggs in a bowl, and beat lightly with a hand mixer.
2. Add the sugar while beating the eggs. Add the cream cheese, vanilla extract, sugar together and mix for 3 minutes gently. Beat the cheesecake filling properly!
3. Sure, there are no big lumps.
4. Next, pour the mixture into the crusted spring-form pan.
5. Put to bake, in a preheated oven for an hour at 375 degrees F.
6. The baked dough done jiggled in the middle.
7. Now, removed the cheesecake, and turns the oven's temperature to 450 degrees F. Get ready to add the topping.

TOPPING:

1. Mix sour cream, pineapple's juice and sugar together.
2. Mix properly and then evenly spread on top cheesecake.
3. Now, put cheesecake back in oven for 5 minutes.
4. When that time completed, allow cooling for an hour before cutting.
5. After that, cover properly; refrigerate for at least three hours.
6. Jamaican Cheesecake Pineapple is ready to serve.
7. I froze this cheesecake for three months. Every time I felt for a slice, I cut one, which is once in two weeks. This cake is delicious to eat frozen. Serve slices for 12 people.

6

CARIBBEAN PLAIN CAKE

The secret to making your cake taste delicious is to use flavorful butter. I am against using butter. However organic is best.

To bake birthday cake you can use plain cake recipe. For me, carrot cake makes delicious birthday cake. I used coconut milk in this plain cake and in all cakes. I believed a cake becomes Jamaican because we over beat the dough hard.

CARIBBEAN PLAIN CAKE

Ingredients:

- 3 cups of flour (all purpose or cake flour)
- 2 tablespoons of baking powder
- 1 teaspoon of sea salt
- 1 cup of butter (real flavored butter makes delicious cake)
- 2 cups of sugar (brown or white)
- 4 eggs (lighter cake if beaten)
- 1 cup of coconut milk, or cow's milk
- ½ teaspoon of white vinegar (distorts spoilage use with coconut milk only)
- 2 teaspoons of vanilla extract

Instructions:

1. Cut two greased papers to size 8.5 to a 9-inches diameter-baking pan.
2. Greased baking pan, and lay papers. Put aside.
3. Sift the flour with the baking powder, and salt. Put aside.
4. Now, dice the room temperature butter, and add the sugar. Use a wooden spoon; cream together.
5. Next, beat the eggs with the vanilla extract, and add the coconut milk with a drop of white vinegar. (Using the white vinegar distorts spoilage for one week).
6. Now add the egg mixture to the butter mixture.
7. Next, add the flour mixture to the creamed butter.
8. Use a mixer, or a wooden spoon to beat the dough properly.
9. After that, pour dough into baking-pan.
10. Lift and dropped, two to six times releases the air bubbles.
11. Bake for 55 minutes in a preheated oven at 350 degrees F., using 8.5 to 9 inches baking pan. Do not over bake.
12. Insert toothpick if it is clean, you are finished. Allow cooling, before removing cake from the pan. Score between cake and baking pan.
13. Flip baking pan with cake over, use your palm to hold the surface of the cake, removed greased papers, and then place on plate slice serve 24 people. Keep refrigerated for 5 days freshness.

7

CARIBBEAN POUND CAKE

Caribbean pound cake

Jamaican pound cake

I know! This pound cake is not traditional. I changed it by adding nutmeg and used coconut milk. Now, my bake-book introduces Caribbean pound cake to you. America is where I first tasted a delicious slice of pound cake.

CARIBBEAN POUND CAKE

Ingredients:

- 3 eggs (large)
- 1 1/3 cups cake flour
- 1 teaspoon baking powder
- ¼ teaspoon sea salt (any is good)
- ¾ cup sugar (granulated)
- 1 ¼ teaspoons vanilla extract
- ¼ teaspoon of nutmeg (grated)
- ¼ teaspoon of almond flavoring (optional)
- 3 tablespoons of coconut milk (or cow's milk)
- 13 tablespoons of butter (real unsalted flavored butter makes delicious cake)
- 1 drop of white vinegar distorts spoilage if using coconut milk

Instructions:

1. Cut two greased papers to size baking pan, which is 4.5 x 12 inches loaf pan.
2. Greased the baking pan, and lay the papers. Put aside.
3. Sift the flour with the baking powder, grated nutmeg, and salt. Put aside.
4. Now, dice the room temperature butter, and add the sugar. Use a wooden spoon and cream together.
5. Next, beat the eggs with the vanilla extract, almond flavoring, and add the coconut milk with a drop of white vinegar. (Using the white vinegar distorts spoilage for one week).
6. Cream the egg mixture to the butter mixture.
7. Then, add the flour mixture to the creamed butter.
8. Use a mixer to beat the dough for 2 minutes.
9. After that, pour dough into loaf-baking pan.
10. Lift and dropped, two to three times releases the air bubbles.
11. Bake for 40 minutes in a preheated oven at 350 degrees F., for the baking loaf I am using.
12. If you use 9 x 5 inches baking pan bake it for 25 to 35 minutes.
13. Insert toothpick if it is clean, you are finished.
14. Allow to cool for 10 minutes before removing cake.
15. Use knife score between cake and baking pan.
16. Slice serving 12 to 18 people. Keep out for a day, and then put in refrigerator sealed for 5 days freshness.

8

CARROT PEANUT CAKE

Carrot peanut cake

Carrot peanut cake is delightfully delicious

To be honest, my carrot cake is with nutty twist. Carrot cakes' delicious flavor makes great birthday cakes in Jamaica.

CARROT PEANUT CAKE

Ingredients:

- 4 eggs (beaten)
- 1 ½ cups sugar (granulated)
- 2 cups flour (all purpose)
- 1 cup coconut oil (any good one is best)
- 2 teaspoons vanilla extract
- 1 ½ teaspoons cinnamon powder
- ¼ teaspoon of nutmeg (grated)
- 1 teaspoon baking soda
- 1 ½ teaspoons baking powder
- ½ teaspoon sea salt (any is good)

CREAM CHEESE GINGER FROSTING:

- 2 cups of icing sugar (powdered sugar, confectioners sugar)
- 8 ounces of cream cheese (room temperature)
- ¼ cup of butter (unsalted room temperature)
- 1 teaspoon of vanilla extract
- 3 to 4 tablespoons of gingers' juice (ounce piece blend with water and strained for the juice only)
- ¼ cup of roasted peanuts (crushed)

For this recipe, you only need half the ingredients to frost this cake.

Instructions:
1. Preheat oven to 350 degrees F. (or 180 degrees C) 8 to 10 minutes before baking.
2. First, lightly buttered and line two 7.5-inches baking pans with each two greaseproof papers.
3. Sift flour, baking powder, soda, cinnamon powder, grated nutmeg, and the sea salt. Put aside.
4. Strip, washed, and grate the carrots finely.
5. Use an electric mixer on low speed to beat eggs for one minute in a bowl. Partially add the sugar while mixing.

6. Cream the room temperature eggs with sugar by beating for 3 minutes, on low speed. (If you use high speed, it will foam and you do not want that happen.)
7. Add the coconut oil, and then vanilla extract, mix properly for one minute on low speed.
8. Now, add the flour mixture, and stir in properly.
9. After that, use plastic spatula gently folds the grated carrots.
10. Now, pour into two separate baking pans, equally.
11. Bake 350 degrees F. for 30 minutes.
12. Insert toothpick in center, it should comes out with just a few moist crumbs.
13. Do not over-bake!
14. After the cakes cools, use a knife to score between around the cake and baking pan; removed cakes easily. Remove the greased papers.
15. Now, you are ready, add frosting to the cakes.

CREAM CHEESE GINGER PEANUT FROSTING

1. First, add the butter and the cream cheese in a large bowl Mix with an electric hand mixer on low speed properly.
2. Second, partially sift the lump free powdered sugar over that. Mix smooth!
3. After that, add vanilla extract, and gingers' juice. Mix properly!
4. Next, use spatula to add frosting between the cakes.
5. Spread frosting on the top, and then sprinkle crushed nuts.
6. Add the second cake, pour more frosting, and then sprinkle more nuts on top.
7. You are finished. Cut to slice and serve.
8. Enjoy Jamaica's carrot peanut ginger cake.
9. Slice serving 12 to 18 people. Keep sealed in refrigerator for 5 days freshness.

9

CASSAVA PUDDING

Caribbean people, uses the cassava root to make many food items. Cassava pudding is not popular in Jamaica. The cassava root is popular in the Caribbean. The way I baked cassava pudding made it looked like a cake on a pudding.

For cassava pudding cake, use my method for this result.

Cassava pudding with raisins

CASSAVA PUDDING

Ingredients:

- 1 ½ pounds cassava roots (grated fine)
- ½ cup brown sugar
- 1 cup flour
- ½ cup cornmeal
- 2 cups coconut milk, or cow's milk
- ½ cup raisins
- 2 teaspoons vanilla extract
- 1 teaspoon nutmeg (grated)
- ½ teaspoon cinnamon powder
- 1 teaspoon mixed spices, or all spices
- ½ cup water
- 1 teaspoon sea salt (any is good)
- 1 teaspoon baking powder
- 1 teaspoon baking soda
- 1 teaspoon coconut oil, or melted butter)

TO CREAM THE TOP

- Add together ½ cup of coconut and cow's milk, add sugar, cinnamon powder, and stir properly. Pour on top cassava dough, before baking.

Cassava Pudding Coffee Sauce Topping

Ingredients:

- 1 teaspoon of coffee
- Some condensed milk
- 6 tablespoons of white rum (any rum is good)

Instructions:

1. If you soaked the raisins, it is best.
2. Cut two pieces of greased papers to the size-baking pan you are using.
3. Next, grease the pan with butter or oil. Then lay the pieces of greased papers flat inside the baking pan.

4. Now, sift flour, cornmeal, mixed spices, salt, and the grated nutmeg into big bowl. (Add all dried ingredients) together, followed the grated cassava root.
5. Add sugar, soaked raisins, cornmeal with the milk along other ingredients.
6. Use a wooden spoon combined properly with love.
7. Next, add dough to the greased baking pan.
8. Lift dropped baking-pan two or three times to release air bubbles from mixture.
9. Cover it; use the baking pan's lid.
10. Alternatively use foil, or a pot's lid, that has no plastic on it.
11. Next, put it on middle rack in the oven.
12. Bake in preheated oven at 350 degrees F.
13. Then set your timer for an hour 35 minutes.
14. Use diameter baking-pan size: 8.5 inches with a lid.
15. If you are using 7 inches pan the time is 45 minutes.
16. Baking times precise, not less, burned if more.
17. When the cassava pudding bakes allow cooling. Use a knife score between the pudding's sides of baking pan.
18. Turn upside down; lay it on a plate.
19. Cassava Pudding is good out for one day. Please refrigerate for 4 days. It tastes nicer chilled to me.

Slice serving 12 to 18 people. Keep sealed in refrigerator for 4 days freshness.

Cassava cake pudding

10

CHEESECAKE

Cheesecake is delicious, nevertheless I can only eat two slices at anyone time.

Cheesecake

Add your favorite fruit like sliced bananas, or strawberries on whipped cream. Traveling Jamaicans introduced cheesecake to Jamaica. Anything Jamaicans love, we adopted and made our own.

Cheesecake baked with Jamaican cream crackers

CHEESECAKE

Ingredients:

CRUST:
- 1 ½ cups of Jamaican cream crackers, or Graham cracker crumbs
- 6 tablespoons of butter (melted)
- ¼ cup of sugar (granulated)
- ¼ teaspoon of nutmeg (grated)

TOPPING:
- ½ cup of sour cream
- 1 tablespoon of sugar (granulated)
- Sliced ripening bananas, or strawberries (optional)

FILLING:
- 1 teaspoon of vanilla extract
- 1 pound of cream cheese
- 2/3 cup of sugar (granulated)
- 4 eggs (large, and beaten slightly)

Instructions:
CRUST:
1. First, greased an 8 inches spring-form pan.
2. Mix crumble crackers with sugar and butter in a large enough bowl.
3. Next, pour the mixture into the greased spring-form pan.
4. Use your fingers spread press crust into spring-form pan.
5. Press crust against the sides and bottom of the pan firmly.
6. Now, put the spring-form pan with compressed crust in refrigerator for 5 to 8 minutes will get crust firm.

FILLING:
1. Now, add eggs beaten lightly in a bowl, with a hand mixer.
2. Add half sugar while you beat the eggs. Add the cream cheese, vanilla extract, and sugar together; gently mix for 3 minutes. Beat the cheesecake filling properly! Be sure there are no big lumps.
3. Next, pour the mixture into the crust.
4. Put to bake, in a preheated oven for 45 minutes at 350 degrees F.
5. You can wait until serving for drizzling glaze, or add whipped cream on each slice, place cherry on top, if you wish.
6. Slice serving 12 to 15 people. Keep sealed in refrigerator for 3 days freshness freeze for two weeks.

11

CHOCOLATE-LAYERED CAKE

Chocolate, coffee, cinnamon and nutmeg bakes delicious chocolate cake.

The moment this chocolate-layered cake went in my mouth it melted like chocolate ice cream. To serve this chocolate cake with vanilla ice cream is my ideal for dessert.

CHOCOLATE-LAYERED CAKE

Ingredients:

- 1 ¾ cups of flour (all-purpose)
- 2 cups of sugar (granulated)
- ¾ cup of cocoa powder (natural and unsweetened)
- 1 ½ teaspoons baking soda
- 1 ½ teaspoons baking powder
- ½ teaspoon of sea salt (any is good)
- ½ teaspoon of cinnamon powder
- ¼ teaspoon of nutmeg (grated)
- 2 eggs
- 1 cup of water or coffee (although coffee is best)
- 1 cup of coconut milk (any milk is good)
- ½ cup of coconut oil (any oil is good)
- 1 ½ teaspoons of vanilla extract

CHOCOLATE FROSTING:

- 6 ounces of chocolate chips (lightly sweetened)
- 1 cup or 1 stick of butter (unsalted and room temperature)
- 2 cups of powdered or icing sugar (sifted)
- 1 ½ teaspoons pure vanilla extract

- Alternatively, buy ready-made frosting from the supermarket.

Instructions:

1. Preheat oven to 350 degrees F. (or 180 degrees C) 10 minutes before baking.
2. First, lightly buttered and line two - 7.5 inches baking pans each with two greased papers.
3. Sift the flour, baking powder, soda, and cinnamon powder, grated nutmeg, salt, and cocoa powder. Put aside.
4. Cream the room temperature butter with sugar.
5. After that, add an egg, mix each properly between eggs.

6. Add coffee grains to mixture. Add the coconut milk (or cow's milk), vanilla extract, and stir in.
7. Next, add the flour mixture. Stir in properly. Use mixer blend the dough smooth. The chocolate cake's dough will be thin.
8. Now, pour into two separate baking pans, equally.
9. Bake at 350 degrees F. just until set in the middle, at 38 minutes. If you used an 8.5 inches baking pan the time will be 27 minutes.
10. Insert toothpick a few moist crumbs is fine. Do not over-bake!
11. Allow cakes to cool.
12. To avoid the cake from deflating turned it upside down between two loaf-baking pans, leaving surface free from touching.
13. After cakes cools, use knife to score between cake baking-pan. Flip to remove the cakes. Remove the greased papers.
14. Now, you are ready, add the frosting to the cakes.

FROSTING:

1. Melt butter and chocolate chips in a cooking pot on low heat.
2. Add the vanilla. Stir in properly.
3. Now, sift the powdered sugar onto the mixture.
4. Use your mixer to beat it properly.
5. After that, use spatula adds frosting to the cake.
6. Add the second cake and continue frosting, until the cake covers with chocolate frosting.
7. If you do not want to make your own frosting, buy from nearest supermarket.

Slice serving 18 to 24 people. Keep sealed in refrigerator for 4 days freshness.

12

CHOCOLATE RASPBERRY MARBLE CAKE

Marble cake smells raw to me; nevertheless, I have ways to bake chocolate raspberry marble cake that is not raw. Prepare eggs last, that is my secret. Do not allow the dough to stay out too long before baking.

Chocolate raspberry marble cake is delicious with milk. My mother sold marble cake at Kingston's Public Hospital, where she worked in the 80s.

JAMAICAN CAKES

CHOCOLATE RASPBERRY MARBLE CAKE

Ingredients:

- ½ cup of butter (room temperature; real flavored butter makes delicious cake)
- 1 cup of sugar (granulated)
- 2 eggs
- 2 cups of flour (all purpose)
- 1 cup of coconut milk, (or cow's milk)
- 1 teaspoon of vanilla extract
- ¼ teaspoon of cinnamon powder
- ¼ teaspoon of nutmeg (grated)
- 2 teaspoons of baking powder
- ¼ teaspoon of baking soda
- ½ teaspoon of sea salt
- 2 tablespoons cocoa powder
- 2 tablespoons of raspberry or strawberry (food color or natural flavoring) - optional
- 3 to 4 drops of red food coloring
- ¼ teaspoon of white vinegar (distorts spoilage only if using coconut milk)

Instructions:

1. Cut two greased papers to size baking pan, diameter 8.5 inches.
2. Do not greased the baking pan, and lay the papers. Put aside.
3. Sift the flour with the baking powder, soda, grated nutmeg, and salt. Put aside.
4. Now, dice the room temperature butter, and add the sugar. Use a wooden spoon and cream together.
5. Next, beat the eggs with the vanilla extract, and add the coconut milk with a drop of white vinegar. (Using the white vinegar distorts spoilage for one week).
6. Add the egg mixture to the butter mixture.
7. After that, add the flour mixture to the creamed butter.
8. Use a mixer to beat the dough for 2 minutes.
9. After that, divide the dough in three parts. Put the dough in three separate containers.
10. Preheat oven 8 to 10 minutes before baking, good time now.

11. Sift the cocoa powder, and cinnamon powder in one container. Stir in.
12. Next, add the raspberry or strawberry liquid, and then red food coloring, and stir in properly.
13. NOTE: You can divide the dough into two parts, and use just cocoa powder.
14. Now, use large spoon, dollop dough; each flavor in own part of the baking-pan.
15. Lift and dropped, four to five times to released the air bubbles.
16. Bake for 38 to 42 minutes in a preheated oven at 350 degrees F. (175 degrees C).
17. Insert toothpick, if it is clean, you are finished.
18. Allow cooling for an hour, before you remove the cake from the pan.
19. To remove the cake, use knife score between and around the cake and baking pan.
20. Palm the cake with your left hand and flipped upside down.
21. Use your right hand to remove the baking pan, then greased papers. Place a plate on the bottom flipped cake upright.
22. Slice serving 18 to 24 people. Keep sealed in refrigerator for 5 days freshness.

Chocolate raspberry marble cake

JAMAICAN CAKES

13

CHRISTMAS CAKE (FRUIT CAKE)

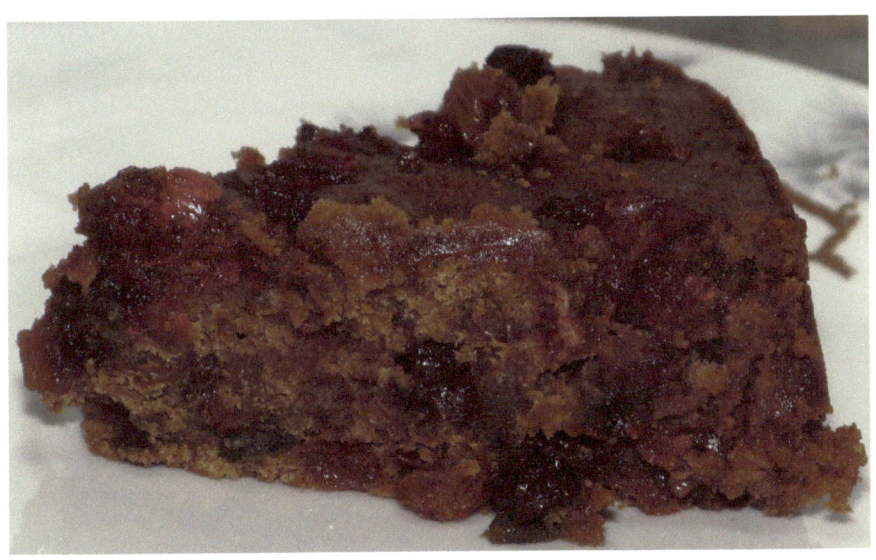

This Christmas cake baked with non-browning.

CHRISTMAS CAKE

Ingredients:

FRUITS (diced or blended)

- 2 pounds raisins
- ½ pound prunes
- ½ pound dates | currants
- 1 pound mixed peel fruits
- 4 cups of red wine
- 7 tablespoons of white rum
- ½ pound cherries (diced)

Note: do not soak the cherries; use it to sprinkle on top just before baking.

BATTER

- 1 pound butter (room temperature)
- ½ pound sugar
- 10 eggs
- 1 teaspoon almond flavoring
- 1 teaspoon vanilla extract
- 1 teaspoon rose water
- 1 pound flour
- 3 teaspoons baking powder
- 2 tablespoons mixed spices, or allspices
- 2 tablespoons of cinnamon powder
- 3 tablespoons of browning (optional)

Note: if add browning, cake would be like pudding. Without browning cake is less dark.

Instructions:

1. Soak diced raisins, mixed peel and prunes fruits in the red wine overnight or at least 3 hours. Some people soaked for weeks.
2. Sure, the fruits diced or blended before soaking in the wine. Remember do not soak the diced cherries.

3. I am using three 8.5 inches diameter baking-pans. Cut two greased papers to size. Then use butter to lightly base all inside the baking pans. Lay the two greased papers on bottom of the baking pans.
4. Get ready to sift together the all dried ingredients, such as the flour, baking powder, mixed spices, cinnamon powder, and grated nutmeg. (Note: do this before the egg mixture. The less time broken egg sits waiting to use, the less cake smells raw.)
5. Cream the butter and the eggs until smooth. Add vanilla extract, almond flavoring, and rose water.
6. Break eggs two at a time, into separate container before adding to the batter. (Do not add eggshells or spoiled eggs.)
7. Now is a good time to preheat your oven at 250 degrees F. Do so 10 minutes before you start baking.
8. Add the egg mixture to the dried ingredients, next browning if using, and then soaked diced fruits raisins prunes with wine.
9. Combine properly by using a wooden spoon are any cake mixer until smooth.
10. Pour the cake batter half way the baking pans.
11. Then lift and dropped each baking pan with dough on a hard surface like a table to release the air bubbles.
12. Next, sprinkle the diced cherries on top before you put it in the oven.
13. For a small baking pan 7 to 8 inches the baking time is 3 hours and 30 minutes.
14. For a larger baking pan 9 to 10 inches the baking time is 4 hours and 30 minutes.
15. Do not open the oven until it is at least 8 to 5 minutes before completion.

Tin slices serve 24 to 30 people. Keep sealed in or out refrigerator for two weeks freshness.

This Christmas cake baked with browning.

14

COCONUT PEANUT CAKE

Caribbean bake-book would not complete without coconut cake. This cake uses for birthday as well.

My coconut peanut cake is original.

COCONUT PEANUT CAKE

Ingredients:

- 1 stick or 1 cup margarine (real flavored butter makes delicious cake)
- ½ cup coconut oil
- 2 cups of sugar
- 5 eggs' yolks
- 5 eggs' whites (beaten heavily)
- 2 cups flour (all purpose)
- 1 teaspoon of baking soda
- ½ teaspoon of sea salt (any is good)
- 1 cup coconut milk (blend ½ teaspoon white vinegar to foam before adding)
- 1 teaspoon vanilla extract
- 1 cup of coconut (shredded)
- 1 cup almond or roasted peanut (mashed)(optional)

Frosting:

- 1 ½ boxes confectioners' sugar (powdered sugar)
- 12 ounces of cream cheese, soft at room temperature
- 1 ½ teaspoons pure vanilla extract

- Some shredded toasted coconut to sprinkle on the top of the cake.

Instructions:

1. Grease lightly with butter two; 9 inches diameter-baking pans, or a 9 x 13 inches pan.
2. Cut two greased papers to the size baking pans. Place them tightly to the bottom.
3. First, blend the coconut milk with ½ teaspoon of white vinegar for 40 second to foam. This helps distorts spoilage.
4. Second, sift all dried ingredients in a large bowl set aside.
5. Third, cream together in a mixing bowl oil and margarine.
6. Add the sugar; use a wooden spoon or mixer to cream the mixture.
7. Add the beaten egg yolks one at a time.
8. Next, add the dried ingredients to liquid.
9. Add the vanilla extract and the blended coconut milk. Stir in with love slowly.

10. Add the shredded coconut and crushed almond or nuts (optional).
11. Fold in the heavily beaten egg whites with spatula.
12. Now, pour the dough half way in the greased baking pans.
13. Then put in preheated oven to bake at 350°F. for 40 minutes. Use a toothpick; test if finished.

Frosting:

- 1 ½ box confectioners' sugar (powdered sugar)
- 12 ounces of cream cheese, soft at room temperature
- 1 ½ teaspoon vanilla extract

- Toast some shredded coconut; sprinkle on top the cake.

Slice serving 18 to 24 people. Keep sealed in refrigerator for 5 days freshness.

15

COCONUT PUDDING

Coconut is my favorite nature's food. This coconut pudding packed with coconut; ate like milk pudding. Strong flavors dissolving my palate like breast milk. Adults would favor coconut pudding, children might like if sweeter. It would be safe to use half cup more sugar baking for children.

Bring coconut pudding to friend's party would make you special.

COCONUT PUDDING

Ingredients:

- 1 ½ pounds coconut (de-shelled)
- 1 cup flour
- ½ cup bread crumbs
- 2 ½ cups water (blended with diced coconut)
- ¼ cup raisins (saved some sprinkle on top)
- 2 teaspoons vanilla extract
- 1 teaspoon nutmeg (grated)
- ½ teaspoon cinnamon powder
- 1 teaspoon sea salt (any is good)
- 1 teaspoon baking powder
- 1 teaspoon baking soda
- 1 teaspoon coconut oil, (or melted butter)
- ¼ cup sugar (granulated)
- ¼ cup icing sugar (powdered sugar)
- 1 tablespoon butter
- ¼ cup condensed milk

Instructions:

1. If you soaked the raisins, it is best.
2. Cut two pieces of greased papers 8 to 9 inches diameter baking-pan with lid.
3. Next, grease the pan with butter or oil. Then lay the pieces of greased papers flat inside the baking pan.
4. Dice coconut then blend with water smooth for 3 minutes; use good blender. (Finely dice few coconuts to add makes pudding interesting).
5. Combine coconut mixture, sugar, vanilla extract, and condensed milk properly.
6. Add dried ingredients by sifting flour, salt, cinnamon powder, with grated nutmeg.
7. After that, add soaked raisins, then use wooden spoon, mix dried with liquid mixture properly.
8. Next, add dough to the greased baking pan.
9. Lift dropped baking-pan two or three times releases air bubbles.
10. Sprinkle, soaked raisins on top dough, before baking. Use the baking pan's lid to cover it. Alternatively use foil, or a pot's lid, that has no plastic on it.

11. Next, put it on middle rack in the oven.
12. Add in preheated oven at 350 degrees F.
13. Then set your timer for an hour 30 minutes.
14. Use diameter baking pan size: 8.5 inches with a lid.
15. If you are using 7 inches pan the time is 45 minutes.
16. Baking times precise, not less, burned if more.
17. When pudding bakes allow cooling, and then use knife to score between the pudding's sides of baking pan.
18. Turn upside down to remove it on a plate.
19. Please refrigerate after cooling sealed for 2 days. It tastes nicer then to me.

Slice serving 15 to 24 people. Keep sealed in refrigerator for 2 days freshness.

16

COFFEE CAKE

My coffee cake is lovely, indeed.
 Delicious coffee cake is a great dessert; breakfast in hurry as well. Enjoy homemade coffee cake with cup of your favorite coffee brand.

 The first time I tasted coffee cake, is when I baked it. The coffee cake is that picture. The molasses blended well with the ingredients. Nevertheless, you can enjoy coffee cake with milk.

COFFEE CAKE

Ingredients:

- 1 ½ cups flour (all purpose and sifted)
- 1 teaspoon baking soda
- 1 teaspoon baking powder
- ½ teaspoon sea salt (any)
- ¼ cup coconut oil (any)
- ¾ cup brown sugar
- ½ cup coconut milk, or cow's milk
- 1 egg (beaten)

Topping:

- 1 tablespoon flour (all purpose)
- 1 teaspoon cinnamon powder
- ¼ teaspoon nutmeg (grated)
- 1 tablespoon butter (melt or not)
- ¼ to ½ cup nuts (mashed), or raisins
- ½ cup sugar (brown)
- 1 teaspoon Molasses - optional

Instructions:
1. Lightly greased 9 x 2 x 5 inches loaf-pan, and lay two greased papers.
2. In a large bowl, combined flour, sugar, melted butter, and mashed nuts. (My method combines all ingredients into a clean plastic bag, or use zip lock bag, do not melt butter this way. This is topping, put aside for later.)
3. Prepare flour first by sifting with baking soda and baking powder etc.
4. Put aside for later! Preheat oven to 375 degrees F, 10 minutes before.
5. Always prepare egg mixture last to avoid raw cake.
6. Now, combine beaten egg, coconut milk with oil.
7. Use wooden spoon or mixer; combine egg, and sifted flour mixture to smoothness. After that, pour dough into baking-pan.
8. Lift and dropped baking pan three to six times releases air bubbles.
9. Then, sprinkle topping all over cake's dough.
10. Bake 25 minutes in preheated oven, toothpick inserted into loaf comes out cleaned. Allow cooling before removing slice for eight people. Keep sealed out 2 days in refrigerator for 3 days freshness.

17

JAMAICAN COFFEE CHOCOLATE CHEESECAKE

Chocolate is my favorite sweet. I love chocolate candy bars, Milo tea, and cocoa tea; I enjoy eating anything with chocolate. Cheese is my second favorite food. Both my favorite foods are in this Jamaican coffee chocolate cheesecake. The blend of coffee, nutmeg, and cinnamon with chocolate makes this cheesecake delicious.

Coffee chocolate cheesecake

JAMAICAN COFFEE CHOCOLATE CHEESECAKE

Ingredients:

CRUST:

- 1 cup of Jamaican cream crackers, or Graham cracker crumbs
- 7 tablespoons of butter (melted)
- ¼ cup of sugar (granulated)

COFFEE COCOA GLAZED TOPPING:

- ¼ cup of butter (melted)
- ½ teaspoon of cinnamon powder
- ¾ cup of sugar (granulated)
- ¼ teaspoon of nutmeg (grated)
- ¼ cup of whipping cream (not whipped cream)
- ¼ cup of cocoa powder (unsweetened)
- ¼ teaspoon of instant coffee
- ½ teaspoon of vanilla extract
- ½ teaspoon of sea salt (any is good)

FILLING:

- 1 teaspoon of vanilla extract
- 1 pound or 12 ounces of cream cheese (softened)
- 1 cup of sugar (granulated)
- 3 eggs (beaten slightly)

Instructions:

CRUST:

1. First, greased an 8 inches spring-form pan.
2. Mix crumbled crackers with sugar and butter in a bowl large enough.
3. Next, spread the mixture into the greased spring-form pan.
4. Use your fingers press crust shape to spring-form pan.
5. Make sure to press crust against the sides and bottom of the pan.
6. Put the spring-form pan with compressed crust in refrigerator for 15 to 20 minutes will get crust firm.

FILLING:

1. First, add eggs in a bowl, and then beat lightly with a hand mixer.
2. Add sugar while you beat the eggs. Add the cream cheese, vanilla extract, and sugar; gently mix for 3 minutes. Beat the cheesecake filling properly! Be sure there are no big lumps.
3. Next, pour the mixture into the crust.
4. Put to bake, in a preheated oven 45 minutes at 350 degrees F.
5. After that, allow cooling before spreading coffee cocoa glazed topping.
6. You can wait for serving to drizzled glaze on one slice, or use a plastic spatula to spread the glaze on top the whole cheesecake.
7. Cover your coffee cocoa cheesecake with the spring form-pan's lid, and put in refrigerator for 12 hours before serving.
8. When ready to serve, add whipped cream, and place a cherry on top, if you wish.

COFFEE COCOA GLAZED TOPPING:

1. Melt butter under low heat.
2. After that, add sugar into bowl.
3. Sift over, the cocoa powder, sea salt, grated nutmeg, cinnamon powder. (Doing this avoids lumps.)
4. Add the whipping cream, melted butter, and vanilla extract.
5. Now, use a hand mixer beat on medium speed 4 minutes, or until thicken. Refrigerate immediately after that maintain thickness.
6. You will use this coffee cocoa glazed topping on the cheesecake.
7. Allow to cool before glazing the cheesecake.

Slice serving eight people. Keep sealed in refrigerator for 3 days freshness.

18

CORNBREAD

My cornbread flavors butter when I used none.

CORNBREAD

Ingredients:

- 1 cup cornmeal
- ¾ cup flour (all-purpose)
- 1 tablespoon sugar
- 1 teaspoon baking powder
- ½ teaspoon baking soda
- ¼ teaspoon sea salt (any)
- 4 tablespoons coconut oil or melted butter
- 2 eggs, (lightly beaten)
- 1 cup coconut milk

Instructions:

1. Greased 9 x 2 x 5 inches baking loaf-pan, cut, and lay two papers.
2. In baking, it is best to prepare egg mixture last, so cake not smells raw.
3. Next, combine flour, sugar, baking powder, baking soda, and the salt. Keep cornmeal in a separate bowl.
4. In another bowl, mix lightly beaten eggs, coconut oil or melted butter, and coconut milk.
5. Now, pour liquid mixture into the flour mixture. Fold few times smooth with some lumps.
6. Add cornmeal, fold until dried mixture dissolves properly, the dough will still be lumpy. Do not over mix!
7. Pour dough into greased loaf baking dish or pan.
8. Bake for 25 minutes; in preheats oven 425 degrees F. until top golden brown. Insert toothpick comes out clean with few dry crumbs.
9. After cooling, score knife between corn bread and pan.
10. Then, flip remove and slice serving eight people. Keep sealed out 1 day in refrigerator for 3 days freshness.

JAMAICAN CAKES

19

CORNMEAL PUDDING

A slice of cornmeal pudding is like having breakfast in hurry.

CORNMEAL PUDDING

Ingredients:

- 2 cups of cornmeal (fine grain)
- ½ cup granulated sugar (for a lightly color pudding)
- ¼ cup flour (any)
- ¼ teaspoon of baking powder
- ¼ teaspoon of baking soda
- 2 cups coconut milk,
- 2 teaspoons vanilla extract
- 1 teaspoon grated nutmeg
- 2 whole pieces of nutmegs' mace
- 1 teaspoon of cinnamon powder (use leaf if got)
- ½ cup of raisins (any dried fruit)
- 2 cups of water
- ¼ cup coconut oil, or (butter)

TO CREAM THE TOP:

- Add together 1/2 cup of coconut and cow's milk, add sugar, cinnamon powder, and stir properly. Pour on top cornmeal dough, before baking.

Cornmeal Pudding Coffee Rum Sauce

Ingredients:

- 1 teaspoon of coffee
- Some condensed milk
- 6 tablespoons of white rum (any rum is good)

Instructions:

1. Combine all the liquid ingredients in a pot for stewing.
2. Add water, coconut milk, salt, sugar, vanilla extract, nutmegs' mace, and raisins.
3. Allow to boil while you stir on low heat.
4. Now, while that boils, combine flour, cornmeal, grated nutmeg, baking powder and soda, with cinnamon powder, all the dried ingredients on one container.

JAMAICAN CAKES

5. Do one of two things at this point.
6. First, sure the stove's flame is gauging very low.
7. One - take half the warmed liquid mixture; use a wooden spoon mix with the flour mixture to dough. Then add to boiling liquid on the stove. To avoid lumps do it this way.
8. Two - Add the dried mixture to the warmed liquid mixture boiling on the stove.
9. Next, stir in properly until thicken, very stiff, not running.
10. Preheat oven 8 minutes before baking.
11. Greased a 9 inches baking pan, Cut two pieces of greased papers to the size baking-pan you are using for easy removal.
12. Remove nutmegs' mace from dough!
13. Pour the thick cornmeal dough into the baking pan.
14. Put to bake for an hour 15 minutes at 350 degrees F.
15. Allow cooling before serving.
16. Jamaican Cornmeal Pudding nice served with coffee rum sauce.
17. Jamaican Cornmeal Pudding is good out for one day. It is because you used coconut milk. Refrigerate no more than 4 days.

Slice serving 12 to 24 people. Keep sealed out 1 day in refrigerator for 3 days freshness.

Cornmeal Pudding

20

EASTER BUN WITH STOUT

Many Jamaicans eat Easter bun with cheese Easter Season. If you are child of Jamaica, you must remember the holidays.

This homemade Easter bun is not like stores. I baked with dragon stout; please note that you can use any stout for this recipe. One person commented on my You-tube Channel Jamaica Bakes, that they used oatmeal stout.

EASTER BUN WITH STOUT

Ingredients: (for two 5 x 12 inches buns)

- 2 bottles of dragon stout (any stout good)
- ½ cup of sugar
- 2 tablespoons of molasses
- 1 tablespoon of browning
- ½ cup of honey
- 2 tablespoons of guava jam or strawberry jelly
- 4 tablespoons of butter
- 6 ½ cups of flour (all purpose)
- 6 teaspoons of baking powder
- 1 teaspoon of baking soda
- 6 teaspoons of mix spices, or allspices
- 1 teaspoon of nutmeg (grated)
- 2 teaspoons of cinnamon powder
- 1 cup of red wine (Sherry)
- 2 cups of raisins
- 1 cup of mixed peel fruits
- 1 cup of cherries (diced, or whole)

GLAZING:

- 2 tablespoons of butter (melted)
- 1 tablespoon of honey

(This is a non-egg recipe, however if you want use 2 eggs, whisk and add to liquid mixture)

Instructions:

1. First, put raisins, mixed peel, and the diced cherries in any red wine or sherry to soak at least overnight is best.
2. Cut 4 pieces greased papers the size of your baking pans. Greased your baking pan first, and then lay two greased papers inside two "5 x 12 inches" loaf-pans, put aside for later.
3. Second, sift together the flour, cinnamon powder, grated nutmeg, baking soda, baking powder, and mixed spices. (All dried ingredients), and then put aside for later.

4. Third step is, melt, and combine the Dragon Stouts, molasses, honey, sugar, jelly, butter, browning, with sugar together in a pot over very low heat on your stove. Stirring dissolves ingredients.
5. Now, if using eggs whisk and add to liquid mixture, stir in properly.
6. Next, pour liquid mixture into flour mixture and combined. Use a mixer or wooden spoon mix properly.
7. It is best to preheat your oven at least 8 minutes before baking, at 160C or 320 degrees F.
8. After that, pour the bun batter half way into each baking pan. Then lift and dropped the baking pan with dough on a hard surface 8 times, to release the air bubbles.
9. It is optional to sprinkle fruit on top. Nevertheless, place whole or diced cherries.
10. Put baking-pan on the middle racks. Please keep the oven closed within time.
11. Now, set timer for an hour to 15 minutes.
12. After cooling, score the side to remove Easter bun.
13. Next, melt add 2 tablespoons of butter with 1 tablespoon of honey in a cooking pot or use the microwave.
14. Glazed Easter Bun using a food's brush; spread the melted butter honey glaze.
15. Serve with Jamaican cheese. Enjoy!
16. Jamaican Easter Bun is nice with butter.

Slice serving 12 to 15 people. Keep sealed out 2 days in refrigerator for 4 days freshness.

21

EASTER BUN MALTA

Easter bun non-alcoholic with malt
    This homemade Easter bun is not like stores. I baked with Malta drink. I did it because the drinks' nutrient is as stout.

EASTER BUN MALTA

Ingredients:

- 1 bottle of Malta drink (284ml, it is sweet)
- ¼ cup, or no sugar is best (brown)
- 1 tablespoon of molasses
- 1 teaspoon of browning
- ¼ cup of honey
- 1 tablespoon of guava jam or strawberry jelly
- 2 tablespoons of butter
- 3 cups of flour (all purpose)
- ¼ cup of bread crumbs
- 3 teaspoons of baking powder
- ½ teaspoon of baking soda
- 4 teaspoons of mixed spices, or allspices
- 1 teaspoon of nutmeg (grated)
- 1 teaspoon of cinnamon powder
- ½ cup of any red wine (sherry)
- 1 cup of raisins (soaked)
- ½ cup of mixed peel fruits (diced)
- ½ cup of cherries (diced, whole)
- 1 egg (optional)

GLAZING:

- 2 tablespoons of butter (melted)
- 1 tablespoon of honey

Instructions:

1. First, soaked raisins, mixed peel, and some diced cherries in any red wine or sherry at least overnight is best.
2. Cut 2 pieces greased papers the size of your baking pan. Greased your baking pan, and then lay the greased papers inside a 5 x 12 inches loaf-pan, put aside for later.
3. Second, sift all dried ingredients, together like flour, cinnamon powder, grated nutmeg, baking soda, baking powder, mixed spices, and breadcrumbs. Put aside for later.

4. Third step is to combine the Malta drink, molasses, honey, jelly, butter, browning, and sugar together in a pot over very low heat on your stove. Be sure to stir dissolving ingredients.
5. Now, whisk egg and add to liquid mixture, stir in properly.
6. Next, pour liquid mixture into flour mixture and combined. Use a mixer or wooden spoon mix properly.
7. It is best to preheat your oven at least 8 minutes before baking, at 160C or 320 degrees F.
8. After that, pour the bun batter into baking pan.
9. Lift and dropped the baking pan with batter on a hard surface 8 times, to release the air bubbles. Sprinkle whole or diced cherries on top.
10. Put baking-pan on middle racks; keep the oven closed within time.
11. Now, set timer for an hour to 10 minutes.
12. After cooling, score the side to remove Easter bun.
13. Next, is glazing, to do that, melt 2 tablespoons of butter with 1 tablespoon of honey in cooking pot, or in microwave!
14. Use a foods' brush; glazed the entire Easter Bun Non-Alcoholic.
15. This original recipe; you wanted non-liquor Easter bun, well here!
16. Easter Bun traditionally, served with Jamaican cheese, nevertheless nice with butter. Enjoy!

Slice serving 12 to 15 people. Keep sealed out 2 days in refrigerator for 4 days freshness.

Easter bun Malta

22

JAMAICAN HARDOUGH BREAD

Homemade hard dough bread

Practice becomes perfect; I do not bake this Jamaican hard dough bread regularly. Nevertheless, if you doubled the recipe you will get bread big as in stores, not hard to do. Some bread brands ingredients tasted generics. The real flavor is gone. Bake your own bread at home.

JAMAICAN HARDOUGH BREAD

Ingredients: (doubled for 5 x 12 inches bread)

- 1 cup warm water
- 1 pound or 2 cups flour (all purpose)
- In addition, ¼ cup to use on baking board and rolling pin.
- 1 teaspoon of sea salt
- 2 tablespoons sugar (granulated)
- 2 teaspoons instant yeast
- 4 tablespoons or ¼ cup of butter

Instructions:

1. First, grease 9 x 2 x 5 inches loaf-baking pan with butter lightly, along with an empty bowl. Put aside for later!
2. Add the yeast to warm or room temperature water until dissolves.
3. Combined all dried ingredients into bowl. Mix in properly!
4. Now, knead butter, flour mixture to crumble into bowl. Using your fingers is best.
5. Next, add yeasted water to buttered flour mixture. Knead to dough!
6. Put the dough into buttered empty bowl. Rub butter on dough properly.
7. Cover properly with clean dry kitchen towel for 25 minutes swelling dough.
8. After that, place dough on floured baking board using ¼-cup flour more.
9. Use hands and fingers knead fold over dough for 15 minutes releases carbon dioxide gas. Use right mixer if have.
10. Now, rub butter on dough, and then place back into greased bowl, 45 minutes for more proofing.
11. On same baking board place dough, use rolling pin to form rectangular shape with the dough.
12. Roll the dough tightly with your fingers forming log shape. Do this, as you would roll up a sleeping bag for storage.
13. Fold corners inside the dough as you roll it tightly.
14. Next, place log shaped dough tightly in the greased loaf pan.
15. Put in dry place; allow dough to proof for 40 minutes. This also removes the extra carbon dioxide gas.
16. After all that, bake for 25 minutes at 375 degrees F. Allow cooling!
17. Slices served eight people. Keep sealed out 3 days in refrigerator for 3 days freshness.

23

MIQUEL'S JAMAICAN GINGER CAKE

Gingers benefits are numerous. This cake is a great way to enjoy ginger. Eating ginger cake comforts me with tea any time of the day.

If you like bulla, you love this ginger cake. I decided adding to bakebook. It is new, I liked it, you will too.

MIQUEL'S JAMAICAN GINGER CAKE

Ingredients:

- 110g or 1 stick of butter
- ½ cup of brown sugar
- 1 tablespoon molasses
- 1 cup of coconut milk
- 1 large egg
- 2 cups of all purpose flour (or baking)
- 1-teaspoon ground cinnamon
- 1-teaspoon ground nutmeg
- pinch of sea salt (any is good)
- ½ teaspoon baking soda
- ½ teaspoon baking powder
- 2 ounces piece of ginger – (peeled, diced) blended with coconut milk and strained.

Instructions:

1. Cut two greased papers to 8 inches diameter baking pan; buttered lightly and lay the greased papers.
2. Blend peeled ginger and coconut milk then strained.
3. Dissolve molasses with the coconut milk. Keep refrigerated until you are ready to use.
4. Combine the butter, sugar to cream, add the egg, then coconut milk.
5. Preheat oven at 150°C or 300° F. 10 minutes before baking.
6. Sift flour, salt, cinnamon powder, grated nutmeg, the baking powder, and soda.
7. Combine all the ingredients properly to smooth texture.
8. Pour dough in the baking-pan.
9. Bake for 45 to 50 minutes. Insert toothpick comes out cleaned with few dried crumbs.
10. Ginger cake is delicious with tea for lunch or at night.
11. Slice serving 8 to 12 people. Keep sealed out a day in refrigerator for 4 days freshness.

24

OLD FASHION EASTER BUN WITHOUT STOUT

Old fashion Easter Bun is like stores. I baked with yeast non-alcoholic.

OLD FASHION EASTER BUN without stout

Ingredients: (for two 5 x 12 inches buns)

- 2 cups of water
- 1 tablespoon instant yeast (1 pack)
- ½ to ¾ cup of sugar
- 4 tablespoons of molasses
- 1 tablespoon of browning
- ½ cup of honey
- 2 tablespoons of guava jam or strawberry jelly
- 4 tablespoons of butter
- 6 cups of flour (all purpose)
- ½ cup of bread crumbs
- 6 teaspoons of baking powder
- 1 teaspoon of baking soda
- 6 teaspoons of mixed spices, or allspices
- 1 teaspoon of nutmeg (grated)
- 2 teaspoons of cinnamon powder
- 1 cup of any red wine (sherry)
- 2 cups of raisins
- 1 cup of mixed peel fruits
- 1 cup of cherries (diced, or whole)

GAZING:

- 2 tablespoons of butter (melted)
- 1 tablespoon of honey

(This is a no egg recipe, however if you want use two eggs, whisk and add to liquid mixture).

Instructions:

1. First, soak raisins, mixed peel, and the diced cherries in any red wine or sherry at least overnight is best.
2. Add instant yeast with 1/4 cup sugar in the 2 cups of water until dissolved properly.

3. Cut 4 pieces greased papers the size of your baking pans. Greased your baking pan first, and then lay two greased papers inside each "5 x 12 inches" loaf-pans, put aside for later.
4. Second, sift dried ingredients, like flour, cinnamon powder, grated nutmeg, baking soda, baking powder, breadcrumbs, and mixed spices. Put aside for later.
5. Third step is to combine the yeast water, molasses, honey, sugar, jelly, butter, browning, and sugar together in a pot over very low heat on your stove. Stir in dissolving ingredients.
6. Now, if using eggs whisk and add to liquid mixture, stir in properly.
7. Next, pour liquid mixture into flour mixture and then combined. Use a mixer or wooden spoon mix properly.
8. It is best to preheat your oven at least 8 minutes before baking, at 160C or 320 degrees F.
9. After that, pour the bun batter half way in each baking pan.
10. Use paper towel, clean any dough on surface or the sides of baking-pans. It will burn first if you do not, as well the scent of burn while bun bakes.
11. Lift and dropped the baking pan with batter on a hard surface 8 times, to release the air bubbles.
12. It is optional to sprinkle fruit on top; nevertheless, decorate it.
13. Place baking-pan on the middle racks, keep oven closed within time.
14. Now, set timer for 55 minutes to an hour.
15. After cooling, score the sides removed Easter bun.
16. To glaze is melt 2 tablespoons butter mixed 1 tablespoon of honey in cooking pot or use microwave.
17. Use a foods' brush to gaze the entire Easter Bun.
18. Serve with Jamaican cheese. Enjoy!
19. Jamaican Old Fashion Easter Bun without stout is nice with butter.

Slice serving 12 to 15 people. Keep sealed out 3 days in refrigerator for 3 days freshness.

25

PINEAPPLE UPSIDE DOWN APPLE SHORTCAKE

Melt in your mouth pineapple upside down apple shortcake

Pineapple upside down apple shortcake

PINEAPPLE UPSIDE DOWN APPLE SHORTCAKE

Ingredients:

- 1 + 1/3 cups of flour
- 1 cup of sugar (granulated)
- 1/3 cup of shortening
- ¼ cup butter or margarine
- 1 ½ teaspoons of baking powder
- ½ teaspoon of sea salt (any is good)
- 2/3 cup of brown sugar
- 9 pineapple slices from juice (in 14 ounces canned), drained
- Jamaican apple (dice to the size of a cherry, or use cherry)
- ¾ cup coconut milk, (or cow's milk)
- ¼ teaspoon of white vinegar (use only with coconut milk)
- 1 egg

Instructions:

1. I am using a 10 inches square baking-pan. Baking dish is best.
2. Add the melted butter into baking pan.
3. After that, sprinkle half the brown sugar evenly over melted butter.
4. Place the pineapple slices evenly apart. Place the diced Jamaican apple in the center of each pineapple slice. Sprinkle other half sugar!
5. First, sift flour, baking powder and the salt in a large bowl. Put aside.
6. Cream the butter, shortening, and granulated sugar in a separate bowl, use a wooden spoon or spatula, add egg, and the coconut milk. Mix properly with wooden spoon or electric mixer.
7. Now, add the flour mixture, and then mix properly for 2 minutes.
8. After that, pour the batter over pineapple and apple pieces.
9. The dough will be thick; therefore, using spatula evenly spreads.
10. Bake in 350° F. preheated oven for 55 minutes. Insert the toothpick in the center, if comes out cleaned, you good! Allow cooling.
11. Score between the baking pan and cake, and then places a plate on top.
12. Flip over then carefully remove baking pan from cake.
13. Pineapple upside down cake is nice served warm.
14. Slice serving nine people. Keep sealed out 1 day in refrigerator for 5 days freshness.

Pineapple upside down apple shortcake

Nine pineapples upside down apple shortcakes

26

RUM AND RAISINS CAKE

Rum and raisins cake made with over-proof white rum. Nevertheless, use any rum. The cake will flavored rum used.

My rum and raisins cake is powerful. Therefore, beware you are consuming alcohol; this cake is not for children or pregnant women. This cake serves good on holidays such as Christmas, or for Easter feast.

JAMAICAN CAKES

RUM AND RAISINS CAKE

Ingredients:

- 1 ½ cups of flour, sifted (all-purpose, baking, or cake flour)
- 2 teaspoons of baking powder
- 1 teaspoon of sea salt (any)
- 1 teaspoon of nutmeg flavoring, or grated
- ¾ cup of sugar (granulated)
- ¼ cup of coconut oil (any good oil)
- 2 eggs (beaten)
- ½ cup of coconut milk, cow's milk, or water
- 1 tablespoon of condensed milk (optional)
- 1 to 2 tablespoons of imitation rum flavoring
- ¼ cup of over-proof white rum (Bacardi, or any rum)
- ¼ to 1 cup more white rum (for basing caking after bake)
- ¼ cup of raisins, (or any dried fruit) (soaked)

Instructions:

1. Soak raisins in water. When ready removed water.
2. Cut two greased papers to size 9 x 2 x 5 inches baking pan. Grease baking pan, and lay flat papers. Put aside.
3. First sift flour than measure 1 ½ cups. Add baking powder, salt, and or grated nutmeg. Option to sift second time, can wait to add over wet mixture. Put aside.
4. Now, cream oil, and sugar, add beaten eggs, vanilla extract, nutmeg, imitation rum flavoring, rum and add the coconut milk or cow's milk.
5. Next, sift flour mixture to the creamed liquid mixture, or sift over it. Use a mixer, or a wooden spoon to beat the dough properly.
6. Pour dough into baking pan.
7. Lift and dropped, two to six times releases the air bubbles.
8. Sprinkle few raisins on top.
9. Bake for 30 minutes in a preheated oven at 375 degrees F.
10. Score, flip baking pan with cake over, and use your palm to hold the surface of the cake, remove greased papers. Sprinkle, pour soak cake with much more rum.
11. A thin slice serves 24 to 30 people. Keep sealed out 2 weeks in refrigerator for 7 days freshness.

27

SPICE BUN

Spice bun with cheese makes nice snack for lunch and dessert.

SPICE BUN

Ingredients:
(Large "5 x12" inches spice bun baking time 50 minutes)

- 5 cups of flour, you might need one more cup (all purpose)
- 1 tablespoon of yeast (instant)
- 1 ¼ cups of coconut milk, or cow's
- 5 ounces of butter (5 tablespoons melted)
- ½ cup of brown sugar
- 1 teaspoon of sea salt (any salt is good)
- ¼ teaspoon of nutmeg (grated)
- ¼ teaspoon of cloves (ground)
- ¼ teaspoon of mixed spices (or allspices)
- 4 tablespoons of mixed peel
- 1 teaspoon of rose water (optional)
- ¼ teaspoon of almond flavoring
- 1 cup of raisins
- 1 tablespoon of cinnamon powder
- 2 eggs (room temperature and beaten)
- 1 teaspoon of white vinegar (use only with coconut milk)

Glaze for the Bun:

- 1 tablespoon of butter (melted)
- 2 tablespoons of honey

Instructions:

1. Soak the raisins in water 1 to 2 hours before you use them. (Do not use that water). This makes raisins taste nice with spice bun.
2. First, sift flour with all spices and the salt in a large bowl.
3. Second, combine the yeast with warmed coconut milk, and add the sugar. Dissolve properly! Add 1-teaspoon vinegar extract, and then blended for 30 seconds. (This will foam the milk, making bun soft, and distorts spoilages for one week.)
4. Third, add the melted butter, almond flavoring, and beaten eggs, to the coconut milk mixture in a separate bowl. Put aside for 10 minutes allow proofing.
5. After that, add the soaked raisins, and mixed peels to the flour proofed dough. Add all ingredients.

6. Now, place dough on lightly floured baking board.
7. Knead dough to soft texture for 6 minutes releases excess gas.
8. Next, grease a separate bowl with butter, and then add the dough into it. Rotate around bowl greasing dough with more butter.
9. Cover with plastic wrap prevents sticking. Then, cover with a cleaned damped cloth. Put in a dry and warm place, it will raise twice the size. Allow it to stay for an hour to 2 hours.
10. After time, knead for two minutes, and then use rolling pin form log loaf. When finished roll dough slightly tight, as you would a sleeping bag; then fold sides inward.
11. Cut two greased papers for 5 x 12 inches loaf-baking pan. Grease the pan then put them in it. Spread more butter on the surface, and then cover with greased paper, which prevents sticking.
12. Now, add the dough in the baking pan. Allow proofing for an hour, rising again.
13. Bake in preheated oven 350 degrees F. for 25 minutes with a small baking pan, and 50 minutes for the larger loaf pan.
14. Allow cooling, and then brush glazed with melted butter and honey.
15. This spice bun is delicious with Jamaican cheese.
16. A thin slice serves 18 to 24 people. Keep sealed out 4 days in refrigerator for day freshness.

Spice bun

28

SPONGE CAKE

Often when telling people I baked, they looked twice, as if saying what special skill. I grew with MomBev, my mother who taught me. Anywhere I travel, it goes with me. Moreover, people love eating my cakes, even in jail.

Sponge cake testes baking skills, it shows how comfortable you are using tools to prepare cake. Following instructions shows attention to details gives great results.

SPONGE CAKE

Ingredients:

- 6 large eggs (white beat to foam)
- Mix eggs' yolk with sugar.
- 1 cup cake flour (sifted first)
- ¼ teaspoon baking powder
- ¼ teaspoon sea salt (any is good)
- 1 cup granulated white sugar (divided)
- 1 teaspoon vanilla extract
- ¼ teaspoon of nutmeg (grated)
- 2 tablespoons water
- 1 teaspoon orange rind (do not used white part)
- ¾ teaspoon cream of tartar

Instructions:

1. Cut two greased papers to size baking pan, which is 8.5 inches diameter baking-pan.
2. Do not grease the baking pan. Put aside.
3. Sift flour with the baking powder, grated nutmeg, and the salt.
4. Now, separate the eggs' white from the yolk.
5. Next, beat the eggs' yolk with 2/3 of the 1 cup of sugar.
6. Add sugar, small portion at a time. Mix until the color brightens looking soft, light yellow, and thick. Use your mixer to beat for 3 minutes.
7. Add vanilla extract, water, and the orange rind only.
8. Beat for a minute on high speed. Put aside.
9. Next, beat eggs' whites with the cream of tartar to foam. While you mixed, add the cream of tartar bit by bit.
10. Add the 1/3 sugar bit by bit while it mixes.
11. Beat until mixture forms morengai; foamed with a peak.
12. Next, add the sifted flour, bit by bit to eggs' white mixture. Use your plastic spatula folds the mixture gently.
13. Now, add the eggs' yolk mixture bit by bit. Fold in gentle and slowly.
14. Pour sponge cake dough into the diameter baking-pan; or use two pieces non-greased tube pan.
15. Lift and dropped four times. You must do this to release air bubbles in the cake's dough.
16. Bake in preheated oven at 350 degrees F. for 35 minutes.

JAMAICAN CAKES

17. To avoid the cake from deflating turned two empty loaf-baking pans upside down on a surface. Then flip cake and lay in middle between the loaf pans.
18. After cakes cool use knife score between cake and baking pan around removes cake easily.
19. A thin slice serves 24 to 30 people. Keep sealed out one week in refrigerator for 2 days freshness.

Sponge cake with Jamaican over-proof rum

Jamaican over-proof rum raisins sponge cake

29

SWEET POTATO PUDDING

Jamaican pudding is not liquid like foreign. Nowhere bakes puddings like Jamaica. Sweet potato pudding delicious flavor is easy to bake. However, labor is intense, why some people try blending ingredients. Nevertheless, do it properly.

Some people add grated yellow yam as well. If doing so use quarter pound fewer sweet potatoes.

SWEET POTATO PUDDING

Ingredients:

- 1 ½ pounds sweet potato (grated equal 2 cups)
- 1 cup brown sugar
- 1 cup flour
- ½ cup cornmeal
- 2 cups coconut milk, or cow's milk
- ½ cup raisins
- 2 teaspoons vanilla extract
- 1 teaspoon grated nutmeg
- ½ teaspoon cinnamon powder
- 1 teaspoon mixed spices, allspices
- ½ cup red wine or water
- 1 teaspoon sea salt (any is good)
- 1 teaspoon baking powder
- 1 teaspoon coconut oil, or (melted butter)

TO CREAM THE TOP

- Add together ½ cup of coconut and cow's milk, add sugar, cinnamon powder, stirring properly. Pour on top sweet potato dough, before baking.

Sweet Potato Pudding Coffee Sauce Topping

Ingredients:

- 1 teaspoon of coffee
- Some condensed milk
- 6 tablespoons of white rum (any rum is good)

Instructions:

1. Peel skin; and washed the sweet potatoes.
2. Grate the sweet potato fine with stainless/aluminum Jamaican, or vegetable grater.
3. Grate or blend the diced coconut with no more than 4 cups of water and squeezed juice using a strainer. Alternatively, use canned coconut milk. (If too thick mix with water!)
4. Soak the raisins in red wine soften it.

5. Cut two pieces of greased papers to the size-baking pan you are using.
6. Next, grease the pan with butter or oil. Then lay the pieces of greased papers flat inside the baking pan.
7. I am using diameter baking-pan size: 8.5 inches with a lid.
8. Now, sift dried ingredients flour, cornmeal, mixed spices, salt, and grated nutmeg in large bowl; add grated sweet potatoes.
9. Add sugar and coconut milk with all ingredients.
10. Use a wooden spoon combined with love. Mix properly!
11. Next, add dough to the greased baking pan.
12. Lift and dropped baking pan three times releasing air bubbles.
13. Cover with baking pan's lid properly.
14. Alternatively use foil, or a pot's lid, that has no plastic on it.
15. Put in preheated oven at 350 degrees F. rack up one from middle.
16. Set timer for an hour 35 minutes.
17. If you are using 7 inches baking pan the time is 45 minutes.
18. Baking times precise, not less, burned if more.
19. When the sweet potato pudding finishes, allow cooling. Use a knife score between the pudding's sides of baking pan.
20. Turn upside down removes it in a plate.

Slice sweet potato pudding serves 18 to 24 people. Keep sealed out 24 hours in refrigerator for 5 days freshness.

Sweet potato pudding

30

TOTO CAKE

Toto Cake is an original, if you are a true Jamaican, tasting Toto, will take you back to childhood.

TOTO CAKE

Ingredients:

- ¼ cup of butter or ¼ stick
- 3 cups of flour
- 1 cup of sugar
- 2 eggs
- 1 tablespoon of vanilla extract
- 1 ½ teaspoons of baking powder
- 1 ½ teaspoons of baking soda
- 1 tablespoon of cinnamon powder
- 1 teaspoon of sea salt
- 1 teaspoon of nutmeg (grated)
- 2 cups of coconut (grated)
- 1 cup of evaporated milk

Instructions:

1. First, grate coconut fine to 2 cups. Put aside until you are ready for it.
2. Sift flour, baking powder, soda, cinnamon powder, and grated nutmeg together in a larger bowl.
3. Second, cream the butter and sugar in a separate bowl.
4. Add eggs and vanilla extract to the butter mixture, and then stir in lovingly.
5. Next, add the shredded coconut. Add the evaporated milk
6. Now, add flour mixture. Stir properly!
7. Pour the dough in a greased loaf-baking pan 8 x 12 inches.
8. Bake for 30 minutes at 400 degrees F. After cools, slice serving eight people. Keep sealed out a day in refrigerator for 4 days freshness.

31

TUTTI FRUITTI CAKE

If not in mood for something big, a simple delicious tutti-fruitti cake is good snack.

Tutti-fruitti cake is popular in Jamaica; children eat tutti-fruitti with milk. I did not eat much cake since making bake-book. Nevertheless, when felt for cake I bought tutti-fruitti cake, once in blue moon.

TUTTI FRUITTI CAKE

Ingredients

- 1 ½ cups of flour, sifted (all purpose, baking, or cake flour)
- 1 teaspoon of baking powder
- 1 teaspoon of baking soda
- ½ teaspoon of sea salt (any)
- ¾ cup of sugar (brown or granulated)
- ¼ cup of coconut oil (any good cooking oil)
- 2 eggs
- ½ cup of coconut milk, or cow's milk
- 1 tablespoon of condensed milk (optional)
- ½ to 1 tablespoon of strawberry flavoring (more is best)
- ½ to 1 tablespoon of pineapple flavoring (more is best)
- 1 teaspoon of nutmeg (grated)
- ¼ to ½ mixed cup of raisins, diced cherries, mixed peel fruits (soak)

Instructions:

1. Dice cherries and soak mixed peel fruits with raisins in water. Use any diced frozen or dried fruit as well, thou optional. (Do not use water, when ready for it removed water). Divide soaked fruits in half.
2. Cut two greased papers to baking pan sized 9 x 2 x 5 inches loaf pan.
3. Greased the baking pan, and lay the papers. Put aside.
4. First sift flour than measure 1 ½ cups. Add baking powder, salt, and grated nutmeg. Alternatively, you cannot sift now again, wait do over liquid mixture. Put aside.
5. Now, combine oil, with the sugar. Mix in with wooden spoon.
6. Add, beaten eggs, vanilla extract, strawberry, and pineapple flavoring. Add half-soaked fruits, and add the coconut milk. Mix in!
7. Next, add sifted flour mixture to the liquid mixture, or sift over it. Use a mixer, or a wooden spoon to beat dough properly.
8. After that, pour dough into baking pan.
9. Lift and dropped, two to six times releases the air bubbles.
10. Sprinkle soaked fruits and raisins on top. Bake for 30 minutes in a preheated oven at 375 degrees F. Keep oven closed within time!
11. Score, flip baking pan with cake over, and use your palm to hold the surface of the cake, remove greased papers.
12. A thin slice serves 18 to 24 people. Keep sealed out 4 days in refrigerator for 2 days freshness.

32

TYPES OF BUTTER, OILS, AND SHORTENING FOR BAKING

Unsalted butter is sweet cream butter as well best for baking. Unsalted butter made from only milk or cream, or both. It contains at least 80 percent milk fat, fatty particles in milk that separated out to make cream.

Salted butter is an original butter and made the same as unsalted butter. It has added salt that people use for spreading on bread. Most recipes call for unsalted butter; therefore, you will not need it.

Organic butter is processed butter made from cows, goat, sheep, or lamp raised without antibiotics. And or growth with hormones, and given 100 percent organic feed grown without toxic pesticides or synthetic fertilizers. It is available unsalted and salted and can be used like conventional butter.

Whipped butter is with air or some other gas, such as nitrogen, adding makes it less dense than standard butter, so little goes a long way. The increased volume results in fewer calories per tablespoon (often half) and a lighter texture. Whipped butter is best for spreading on toast and finishing dishes. I do not recommend this butter for baking nor cooking.

European-style butter is reasons why many people love French croissants. The European-style butter is load with extra milk fat, about 82 to 85 percent for most brands. European-style butter has less moisture than standard butter and so produces extra-flaky pastries and tender, with lovely fluffy cakes. It is made with fermented (also called "cultured") cream, it has a slight tang. European-style butter is use for all cooking tasks.

Spread-able butter is a combination of regular butter and vegetable oil, and sometimes other flavorings and fillers, this product maintains a soft texture even when refrigerated. Spread-able butter is not use for baking or cooking.

Light butter is half the calories of standard butter, and contains 40 percent milk fat, less than most. The other 60 percent made up of water, lactic acid, and other fillers. Do not use light butter for baking nor cooking.

"Butter-Like Spreads" that is marked with the label buttery spread have a similar soft texture for spreading butter; contains 5 percent real butter less sometimes none. Instead, it is makings primarily from a blend of vegetable oils and other fillers. Its benefits include fewer calories, less fat, and just a trace amount of cholesterol; not recommended for baking or cooking.

Butter is a dairy product made by churning fresh or fermented cream or milk, to separate the butterfat from the buttermilk. Generally used as a spread and a condiment, as well as in cooking, baking, sauce making, and pan-frying.

Shortening is a type of solid fat that made from vegetable oils, such as soybean and cottonseed oil. Shortening get its name from shortens gluten strands in wheat adding fat.

"Shortening" processed by a method called hydrogenation. That involves adding extra hydrogen atoms, aforementioned vegetable fats, and turning solid, not liquid. This turns previously un-hydrogenated oil into a partially hydrogenated fat with "trans" fatty acids. Today, shortening made with trans-fat free by fully hydrogenating the oils. Tastes and functions the same way as partially hydrogenated shortenings.

Some cakes recipes instruct to add oil. Numerous oils you can use, such as vegetable oil, coconut oil and corn oil are among the most common and affordable oils available on the market, but are they healthy? The olive oil offers many health benefits, but is it good for baking? Look at popular plant-based oils out there.

Oils flavor can be from sweet and nutty coconut oil to buttery corn oil to grassy and zesty olive oil. Refined oils taste more neutral than their unrefined oils. Sometimes, Olive strong flavor; is better for certain cake, but usually a lighter flavor is preferred.

The important health benefits oils should be high in healthy monounsaturated fats. Oils can also be a great source of polyunsaturated fats like omega-3 fatty acids, which prevent disease, and omega-6 fatty acids, which lower bad LDL cholesterol and protect the heart. Avocado oil and coconut oil can be pricey.

Some consumers are also wary of refined oils that undergo processing with chemical solvents like toxic hexane. Alternatively, oils are extracting from seeds mechanically using extreme pressure with an expeller, or screw press. The product described as cold-pressed, if done in cold temperature.

Baking with olive oil is healthy due to its high level of monounsaturated fats, but olive oil can overpower the taste of your baked goods. Do not bake your cake with extra-virgin olive oil, made using a natural method of extraction for the purest oil, because of its strong flavor and low smoke point, best for drizzling over salads! If you choose to bake with olive oil, choose light olive oil. Undergoes fine filtration process that gives it a lighter flavor and higher smoke point. Processing olive oils significantly diminishes antioxidant value. Compare to other oils, olive oil is expensive.

Corn oil extracted from an oil-rich inner portion kernel called the germ. Refined into flavorless oil with a smoke point of 450°F, great for baking but really shines high-heat cooking like deep-frying. Unrefined corn oil, which tastes buttery, has a low smoke point of 320°F, better suited for dips and salads.

Most, corn oil extracts by expeller and after treated with chemical solvents. Majority of the oils, making is from genetically modified corn. Choose organic and 100% expeller-pressed oils if possible. As for health benefits, corn oil has high levels of polyunsaturated fats, great for lowering blood cholesterol levels, but lower levels of monounsaturated fats than canola oil.

Peanut oil, sunflower oil and safflower oil are other types of oils. You can use them interchangeably in baking recipes for similar results, slight differences texture, and flavor. These oils have high smoke points that are an important factor for baking.

People realizing coconut oil and other coconut-based products have been getting notice. In this bake-cookbook, I use coconut milk and oil often. Coconut works as a great substitute for oil and butter in baking recipes since it tolerates high temperatures. It is a great dairy-free option and is popular with special diets.

Coconut oil very high level saturated fat, lauric acid. Early studies suggest may not be harmful to one's health. However, when compared to other oils, coconut oil offers a little more health benefits making it expensive.

Vegetable shortening is making from vegetable oil, which hydrogenated into a semi-solid state. Vegetable shortening is good for baking, because it can produce flaky pastries and piecrusts. However, it is high in unhealthy Tran's fat, which can raise bad cholesterol, lower good cholesterol and lead to health problems.

Chapter 33
Measurements Equivalents

Set amount:	Equal to:
1/2 teaspoon	= 30 drops
1 teaspoon	= 1/3 tablespoon or 60 drops
3 teaspoons	= 1 tablespoon or 1/2 fluid ounce
1/2 tablespoon	= 1 1/2 teaspoons
1 tablespoon	= 3 teaspoons or 1/2 fluid ounce
2 tablespoons	= 1/8 cup or 1 fluid ounce
3 tablespoons	= 1 1/2 fluid ounce or 1 jigger
4 tablespoons	= 1/4 cup or 2 fluid ounces
5 1/3 tablespoons	= 1/3 cup or 5 tablespoons + 1 teaspoon
8 tablespoons	= 1/2 cup or 4 fluid ounces
10 2/3 tablespoons	= 2/3 cup or 10 tablespoons + 2 teaspoons
12 tablespoons	= 3/4 cup or 6 fluid ounces
16 tablespoons	= 1 cup or 8 fluid ounces or 1/2 pint

Measurements Equivalents:

Set amount:	Equal to:
1/8 cup	= 2 tablespoons or 1 fluid ounce
1/4 cup	= 4 tablespoons or 2 fluid ounces
1/3 cup	= 5 tablespoons + 1 teaspoon
3/8 cup	= 10 tablespoons + 2 teaspoons
5/8 cup	= 1/2 cup + 2 tablespoons
3/4 cup	= 12 tablespoons or 6 fluid ounces
7/8 cup	= 3/4 cup + 2 tablespoons
1 cup	= 16 tablespoons or 1/2 pint or 8 fluid ounces
2 cups	= 1 pint or 16 fluid ounces
1 pint	= 2 cups or 16 fluid ounces
1 quart	= 2 pints or 4 cups or 32 fluid ounces
1 gallon	= 4 quarts or 8 pints or 16 cups or 128 fluid ounces
7/8 cup	= 3/4 cup + 2 tablespoons

34

CONCLUSION

Buy good pans, baking with dish make cake's side clean and pretty. Avoid buying non-stick baking pan that coated with paint usually gray. It is best to buy stainless or aluminum baking pans and utensils for kitchen. If you buy good brand kitchen appliances, you will have a good experience for one, and two your appliances will last a long time. Your kitchen will have character and beauty.

How you can tell if cake is spoil? Homemade cakes made with fresh natural ingredients and often no preservatives. Usually can stay out one day, but must kept refrigerated for two to three day for freshness. Many cakes taste better after two days. If you buy cake from store or bakery and concerned if spoil, do the following. Break the cake in half with hands, and if you see spider web stretches across, or mildew, then cake old and spoiled. If cake tastes old, do not eat, it is developing bacteria and can sicken you.

I really want you to know every cake, pudding and bread recipes all baked by me. Tested and passed by friends, online, You-tube, and persons who bought cakes from me.

I do not buy cakes, nor eat much. Nevertheless, using healthy cooking oils instead butter with coconut milk works for me. Doing this book, I learned butter can be organic and is real food. Who remembered real butter taste? That real flavor of real cow's milk, no additives, which developed good dairy products. Butters today, my opinion are not healthy, whether package said so. Industries are taking natural calories form real food, and then adding unreal vitamins to processed food passing as real food.

Cakes I recommend you bake as gift for parties, friends, or family. Trust me they will appreciate it. Men and women love rum and raisins cake, great for parties and office functions. Coffee cake, banana bread, cheesecake, carrot cake, and chocolate cake as well, and along with black forest cake. Your family would love sweet potato, or cornmeal pudding, banana bread, pineapple upside down apple cake, and Caribbean pound cake.

A special gift for someone, you love whole hearty would be pineapple cream cheesecake, or giving coconut pudding is unique. For men bake any cake with chocolate and nutmeg, that will win him over. Coffee chocolate cheesecake, coffee cake make with peanut in molasses, or chocolate double-layered cake with chocolate frosting does magic.

Why preheat oven before baking? Why keep oven closed while baking? From time cake goes into oven ingredients expands and rise. Therefore, oven must maintain consistent temperature within baking for great result. Precise time bakes cake properly. Keep oven closed maintains temperature. Cake would not deflate, under bake, nor burned.

The less time broken egg sits waiting to use, the less your cake smells raw. Prepare eggs last, that is my secret. Do not allow the dough to stay out too long before baking. Use paper towel, clean any dough on surface or the sides of baking-pans. It will burn first if you do not, as well the scent of burn while the cake bakes.

Gas Mark or Electric Oven Conversion Chart

Gas mark and electric ovens conversion chart. This information was copied form the internet.

Gas Mark or Electric Conversion Chart			
Degrees Fahrenheit to Celsius for Electric or Gas Ovens			
Gas Mark:	Fahrenheit:	Celsius:	Description:
1/4	= 225°	= 110	Very cool / Very slow
1/2	= 250°	= 130	---
1	= 275°	= 140	Cool
2	= 300°	= 150	----
3	= 325°	= 170	Very Moderate
4	= 350°	= 180	Moderate
5	= 375°	= 190	-----
6	= 400°	= 200	Moderately hot
7	= 425°	= 220	hot
8	= 450°	= 230	---
9	= 475°	= 240	Very hot

This chart should be accurate enough for all cooking needs, keep in mind the temperatures vary with different types, brands, sizes of ovens.

AUTHOR | PRIMARY PROPER NUTRITION CHEF

MiQuel Marvin Samuels

MIQUEL MARVIN SAMUELS

Born in Kingston, Jamaica, MiQuel Samuels graduated High School, continued studies in, Maryland USA, and Jamaica. He is professional. He is a phenomenal home chef with great baking skills. He loves literature, art, and music, moreover publishing. MiQuel Samuels is wise, creative, with adventure. He is passion with love for life, Divine and health conscious. His extending continuous knowledge for primary proper nutrition is developing.

Printed in the USA, for
(LiberatePeople.com)
JAMAICA W.I.

www.ingramcontent.com/pod-product-compliance
Lightning Source LLC
Chambersburg PA
CBHW041620220426
43661CB00046B/1513